THERE'S GLORY UNDERNEATH MY SKIN!

Written and Illustrated by

Rebecca Morris

Dedicated to our beautiful daughter

Eliana Rose Zion

To our wonderful son Raphael

All the lights are off, but I'm shining from within!

The light inside of me

is sparkly and bright!

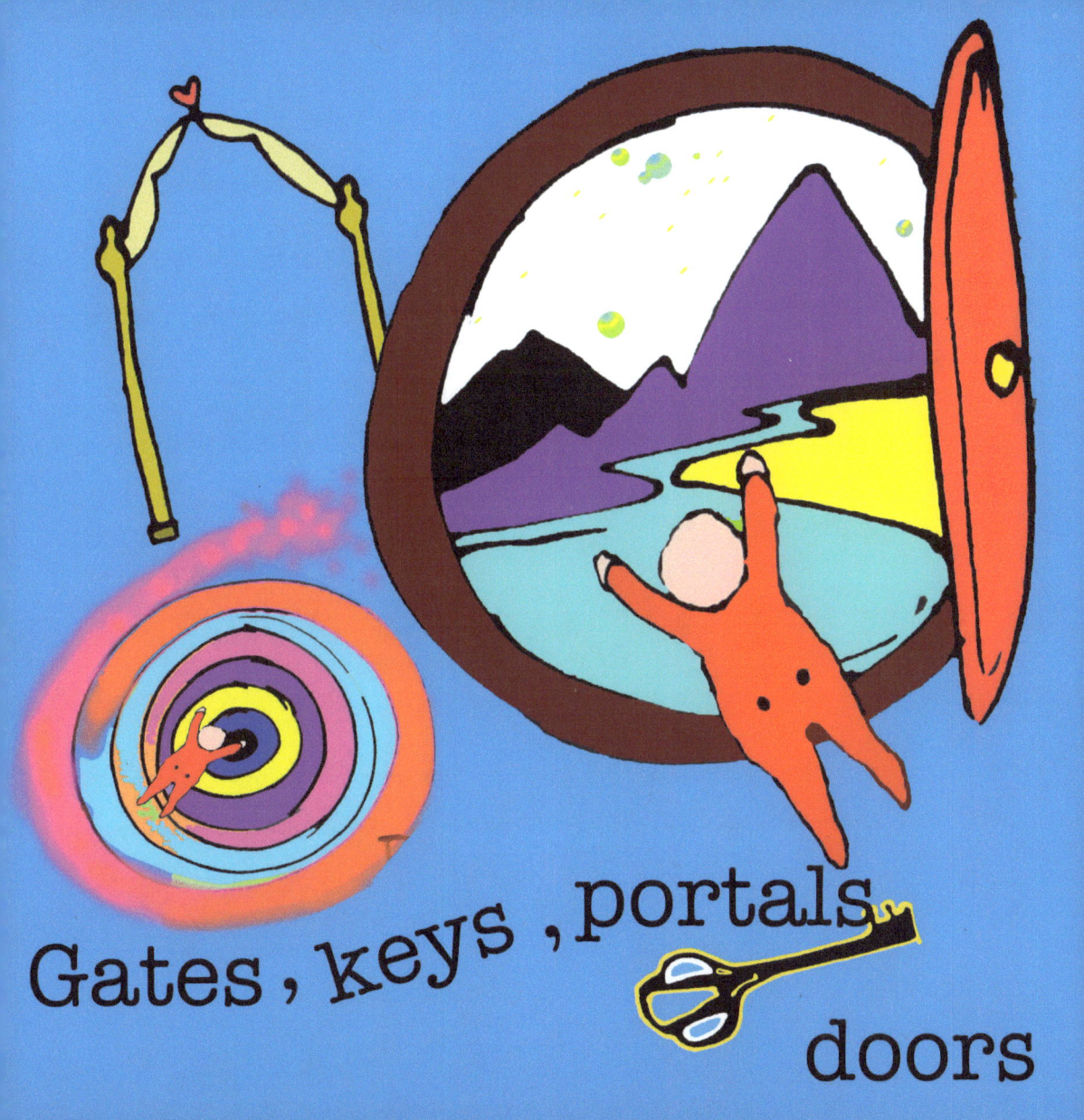

The water's flowing out of my heart,

THE GLORY'S UNDERNEATH MY SKIN!

The mysteries of Heaven,

Treasure for you and me!

Blessings

I bless your dreams.

That the mysteries of the Kingdom would open up around you and engage with you.

It is YOU we love!

I bless you to know how loved you are, even as you sleep.

A huge THANK YOU to the lovely Lindi Masters, Yeye Ikenna and Jane Schroeder for your amazing love and support.

A special thank you to my husband David Morris.

Published by Seraph Creative in 2018
www.seraphcreative.org

All rights reserved. No part of this publication may be reproduced, stored in a retrieval system, or transmitted, in any form or by any means, electronic, mechanical, photocopying, recording or otherwise, without the prior permission of the copyright holder.

© Rebecca Morris 2018

ISBN 978-0-6399841-9-3

www.ingramcontent.com/pod-product-compliance
Lightning Source LLC
Chambersburg PA
CBHW041155290426
44108CB00002B/79